A207
From Enlightenment to Romanticism,
*c.*1780–1830

Illustrations Book

This publication forms part of an Open University course A207 *From Enlightenment to Romanticism c.1780–1830*. Details of this and other Open University courses can be obtained from the Course Information and Advice Centre, PO Box 724, The Open University, Milton Keynes MK7 6ZS, United Kingdom: tel. +44 (0)1908 653231, e-mail general-enquiries@open.ac.uk

Alternatively, you may visit the Open University website at http://www.open.ac.uk where you can learn more about the wide range of courses and packs offered at all levels by The Open University.

To purchase a selection of Open University course materials visit the webshop at www.ouw.co.uk, or contact Open University Worldwide, Michael Young Building, Walton Hall, Milton Keynes MK7 6AA, United Kingdom for a brochure. tel. +44 (0)1908 858785; fax +44 (0)1908 858787; e-mail ouwenq@open.ac.uk

The Open University
Walton Hall, Milton Keynes
MK7 6AA

First published 2005

Edited, designed and typeset by The Open University.

Printed and bound in the United Kingdom by Nicholson & Bass Ltd.

ISBN 0 7492 9647 X

1.2

Contents

VIDEO 3

VIDEO 4

Plate 2.1   Vincenc Morstadt, Theatre of Estates, Prague (also known as the Nostitz Theatre), 1835, pre-etched steel engraving of sepia drawing, 24.3 x 36.4 cm, City of Prague Museum. Photo: Karel Šproutil.

Plate 4.1   Allan Ramsay, David Hume, 1766, oil on canvas, 76.2 × 63.5 cm, Scottish National Portrait Gallery, Edinburgh. Photo: SNPG/Bridgeman Art Library.

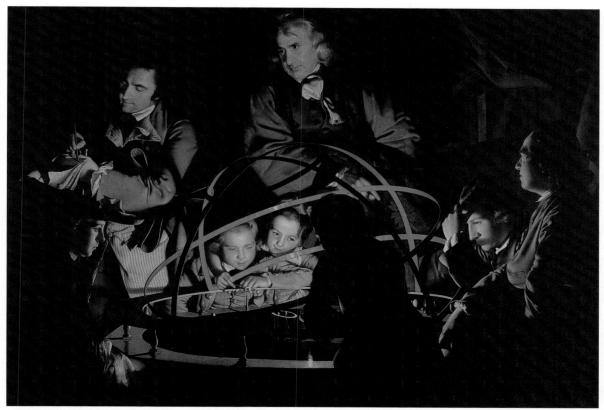

Plate 4.2   Joseph Wright of Derby, Lecture on the Orrery in which a Candle is used to create an Eclipse, *1766, oil on canvas, 147.3 x 203 cm, Derby Museum and Art Gallery. Photo: reproduced by courtesy of Derby Museum and Art Gallery/Bridgeman Art Library/John Webb.*

Plate 4.3   William Blake, Isaac Newton, *c.1795, colour print finished in ink and watercolour on paper, Tate Gallery, London. Photo: © Tate, London 2002.*

Plate 5.1   Allan Ramsay, Jean-Jacques Rousseau, *1766, oil on canvas, 74.9 x 64.8 cm, National Gallery of Scotland, Edinburgh. Photo: reproduced by courtesy of the National Gallery of Scotland, Edinburgh.*

Plate 5.2   Jacques-Louis David, The Death of Socrates, 1787, oil on canvas, 129.5 x 196.2 cm, Metropolitan Museum of Art, New York. Photo: reproduced by courtesy of The Metropolitan Museum of Art, Catherine Lorillard Wolfe Collection, Wolfe Fund, 1931 (31.45). © 1995 The Metropolitan Museum of Art.

Plate 5.3 *Eustache le Sueur,* Christ on the Cross with the Magdalen, the Virgin Mary and Saint John the Evangelist, *c.1642, oil on canvas, 109.5 x 73.8 cm, National Gallery, London. Photo: © The National Gallery, London.*

Plate 5.4   Francisco de Goya, Saturn Devouring One of his Children, *1819–24, oil on canvas, 146 x 83 cm, Museo del Prado, Madrid. Photo: Bridgeman Art Library.*

Plate 6.1 Louis-Léopold Boilly, The Actor Chenard as a 'Sans-Culotte', *1792, oil on panel, 33.5 × 22.5 cm, Musée de la Ville de Paris, Musée Carnavelet, Paris. Photo: Giraudon/Bridgeman Art Library.*

Plate 6.2 Calendar for Year III of the French Republic, *Bibliothèque Nationale de France*, Paris.

Plate 6.3   François Verly, view of the proposed public bath and theatre in Lille, Musée des Beaux-Arts, Lille.
Photo: © RMN/Quecq d'Henripret.

Plate 6.4   Quatremère, group with la Patrie in the centre for the eastern nave of the Pantheon, 1793, Bibliothèque Nationale de France, Paris.

Plate 6.5   Joseph Chinard, bas-relief for the city hall in Lyon, 64 x 54 x 3 cm, Musée des Beaux-Arts de Lyon. Photo: © Studio Basset.

Plate 7.1 *Anonymous,* Allegorical Representation of Napoleon's Achievement, *1810, Bibliothèque Nationale de France, Paris.*

23

Plate 9.1   Jacques-Louis David, The Oath of the Horatii, 1785, oil on canvas, 329.9 × 428.8 cm, Louvre, Paris. Photo: © RMN/G. Blot/C. Jean.

Plate 9.2 Eugène Delacroix, Massacres of Chios, *1824, oil on canvas, 417.2 x 354 cm, Louvre, Paris. Photo:* © RMN/L. Mage.

Plate 9.3 Antoine-Jean Gros, General Bonaparte at the Bridge of Arcole, *1797, oil on canvas, 130 × 94 cm, Musée National du Château, Versailles. Photo: © RMN/G. Blot.*

Plate 9.4   Antoine-Jean Gros, Bonaparte at the Bridge of Arcole, *1796, oil sketch, 72 × 59 cm, Louvre, Paris. Photo: © RMN/G. Blot.*

Plate 9.5   Hyacinthe Rigaud, Marshal Charles-Auguste de Matignon, *1704, 147 x 113 cm, National Arts Centre, Karlsruhe. Reproduced by courtesy of National Arts Centre, Karlsruhe.*

NAPOLÉON BONAPARTE

Bataille d'Arcole gagnée le 25 Brumaire an 5.

Dédié a l'Armée d'Italie

Peint par Gros   Gravé par Piroli

Plate 9.6   Thomas Piroli, *after Gros,* General Bonaparte at the Bridge of Arcole, *1797, etching with aquatint, 72 x 59 cm, Bibliothèque Nationale de France, Paris.*

Plate 9.7   Jacques-Louis David, The Death of Marat, *1793, oil on canvas, 160.7 × 124.8 cm, Musées royaux des Beaux-Arts de Belgique, Brussels. Photo: Cussac.*

Plate 9.8   Jacques-Louis David, Bonaparte Crossing the Alps, *1800–1, oil on canvas, 260 × 221 cm, Châteaux de Versailles et de Trianon. Photo: © RMN/Arnaudet/J. Schormans.*

Plate 9.9   Antoine-Jean Gros, Bonaparte as First Consul, *1802, oil on canvas, 205 × 127 cm, Musée Nationale de la Légion d'Honneur, Paris. Photo: Bridgeman Art Library.*

Plate 9.10   *François Gérard*, Napoleon in his Imperial Robes, *1805, oil on canvas, 227 x 145 cm, Châteaux de Versailles et de Trianon. Photo:* © *RMN/Arnaudet.*

Plate 9.11 Jean-Auguste-Dominique Ingres, Napoleon on the Imperial Throne, *1806, oil on canvas, 260 × 163 cm,*
Musée de l'Armée, Paris. Photo: reproduced by courtesy of Musée de l'Armée, Paris.

Plate 9.12   Jean-Auguste-Dominique Ingres, Bonaparte as First Consul, *1804, 227.5 x 147 cm, Musée d'Art Moderne et d'Art Contemporain de la Ville de Liège.*

Plate 9.13 Jacques-Louis David, The Emperor Napoleon in his Study at the Tuileries, *1812, oil on canvas,*
204 x 125 cm, National Gallery of Art, Washington, DC. Reproduced by courtesy of Samuel H. Kress Collection.
Photo: © 2002 Board of Trustees, National Gallery of Art, Washington, DC.

36

Plate 9.14   Antoine-Jean Gros, The Battle of Nazareth, 1801, oil sketch, 135 × 195 cm, Musée des Beaux Arts, Nantes. Photo: © RMN/G. Blot.

Plate 9.15 Antoine-Jean Gros, Bonaparte Visiting the Plague-Stricken of Jaffa, 1804, oil on canvas, 532.1 × 720 cm, Louvre, Paris. Photo: © RMN.

Plate 9.16 Antoine-Jean Gros, The Battle of Aboukir, 1806, oil on canvas, 578 x 968 cm, Châteaux de Versailles et de Trianon. Photo: © RMN/P. Willi.

Plate 9.17 François Gérard, The Battle of Austerlitz, 1810, oil on canvas, 510 × 958 cm, Châteaux de Versailles et de Trianon. Photo: © RMN.

Plate 9.18 Pierre-Narcisse Guérin, Bonaparte Pardoning the Rebels of Cairo, 1808, oil on canvas, 365 × 500 cm, Châteaux de Versailles et de Trianon. Photo: © RMN/Arnaudet/J. Schormans.

Plate 9.19   Antoine-Jean Gros, Napoleon Visiting the Field of the Battle of Eylau, 1808, oil on canvas, 521 × 784 cm, Louvre, Paris. Photo: © RMN.

Plate 9.20   Louis-Léopold Boilly, Reading the 'Bulletin of the Grande Armée', *1807, oil on canvas, 47 × 60 cm, The Saint Louis Art Museum. Gift of Mr and Mrs R Crosby Kemper through the Crosby Kemper Foundations.*

Plate 9.21   Antonio Canova, Napoleon, *1802, marble, Galleria d'Arte Moderna, Florence. Photo: Bridgeman Art Library.*

Plate 9.22   Charles Meynier, Napoleon Visiting the Field of the Battle of Eylau, 1807, oil sketch, 93 × 146 cm, Châteaux de Versailles et Trianon. Photo: © RMN/G. Blot/J. Schormans.

44

Plate 9.23   Louis-Léopold Boilly, The Conscripts of 1807 Parading Past the Saint-Denis Gate, 1807, oil on canvas, 84.5 × 138 cm, Musée de la Ville de Paris, Musée Carnavelet, Paris. Photo: Bridgeman Art Library.

Plate 9.24 Théodore Géricault, The Wounded Cuirassier, *1814, oil on canvas, 358 × 294 cm, Louvre, Paris. Photo: © RMN/G. Blot.*

Plate 9.25   Jacques-Louis David, The Intervention of the Sabine Women, 1799, oil on canvas, 386 x 520 cm, Louvre, Paris. Photo: © RMN/J. .

Plate 9.26   Anne-Louis Girodet-Trioson, Scene from a Deluge, *1806, oil on canvas, 431 x 341 cm, Musée Magnin, Dijon.*
Photo: © RMN/R.G. Ojeda.

Plate 9.27   Antonio Canova, Napoleon as Mars the Peacemaker, *1803, marble, Apsley House, London.
Photo: Victoria and Albert Picture Library, London/Daniel McGrath/Sara Hodges.*

Plate 9.28   Jacques-Louis David, The Coronation of Napoleon, 1805–7, oil on canvas, 621 x 979 cm, Louvre, Paris. Photo: © RMN/H. Lewandowski.

Plate 9.29   Louis-Léopold Boilly, The Grand Salon of 1808, Viewing the David 'Crowning of Napoleon', 1808, oil on canvas, 60 × 81 cm, Private Collection, New York.

Plate 9.30 Jacques-Louis David, Distribution of the Eagle Standards, 1810, 610 × 931 cm, Châteaux de Versailles et de Trianon. Photo: © RMN/ P. Willi.

Plate 9.31 Anne-Louis Girodet-Trioson, The Revolt at Cairo, 1810, oil on canvas, 365 × 500 cm, Châteaux de Versailles et de Trianon. Photo: © RMN/Arnaudet/J. Schormans.

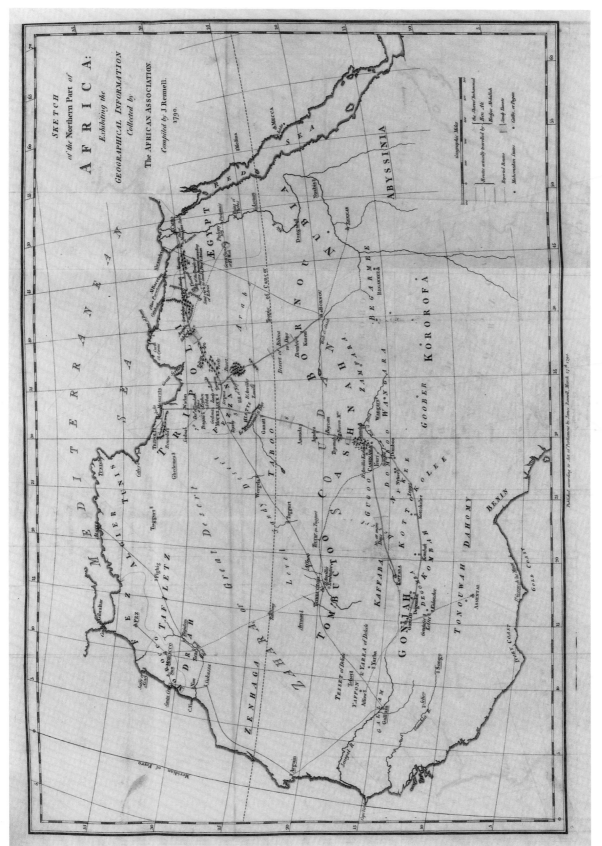

Plate 12.1 James Rennell, Sketch of the Northern Part of Africa: Exhibiting the Geographical Information Collected by the African Association, 1790, British Library, London. Photo: by permission of the British Library, London (shelfmark 454.f.15).

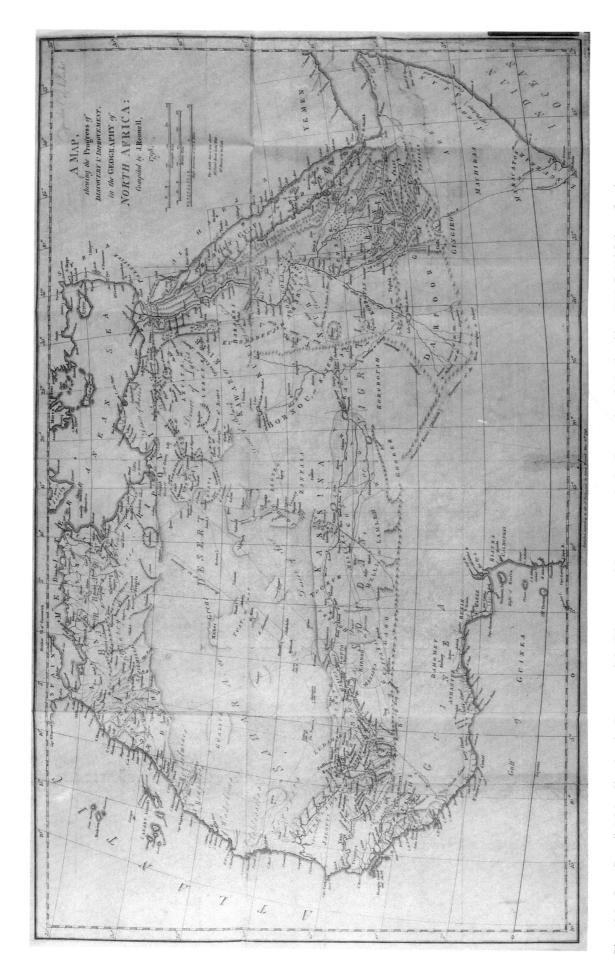

Plate 12.2   James Rennell. A Map Showing the Progress of the Discovery and Improvement in the Geography of North Africa, 1798, British Library, London.
Photo: by permission of the British Library, London (shelfmark 147.e.6).

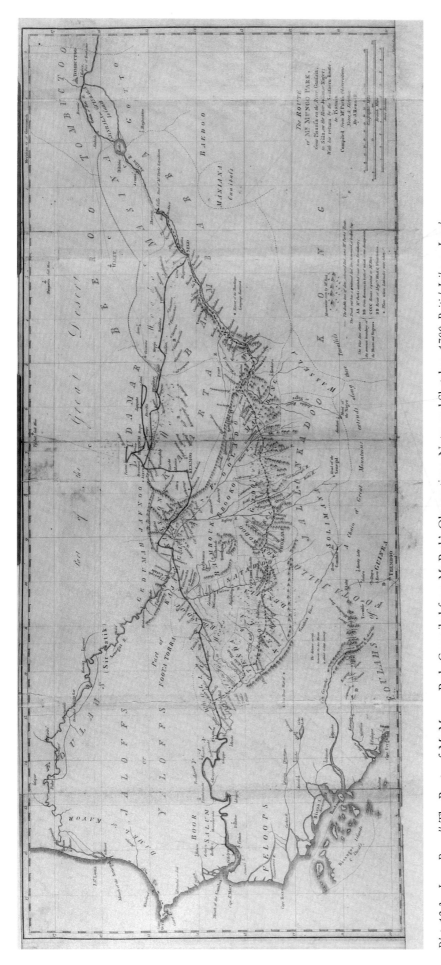

Plate 12.3   James Rennell, The Route of Mr Mungo Park, Compiled from Mr Park's Observations, Notes and Sketches, 1799, British Library, London.
Photo: by permission of the British Library, London (shelfmark 147.e.6).

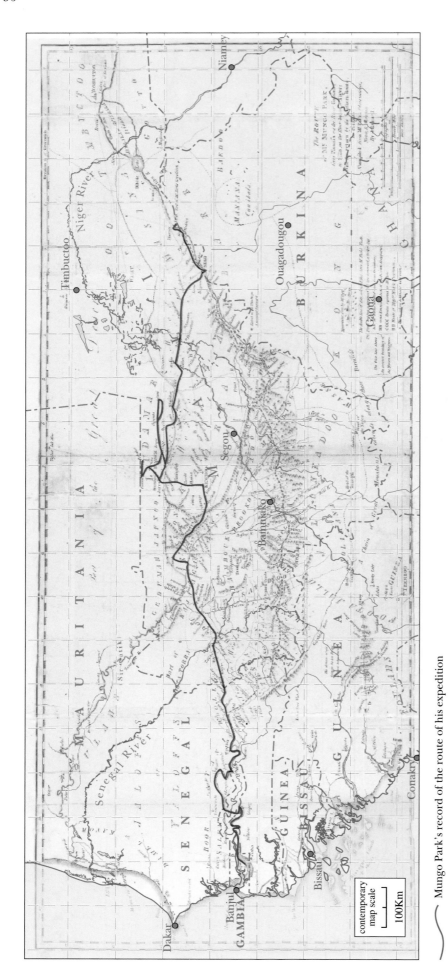

⌒ Mungo Park's record of the route of his expedition

Plate 12.4   Plate 12.3 superimposed with modern boundaries.

Plate 14.1 J.M.W. Turner, 'Slave Ship' (Slavers Throwing Overboard the Dead and Dying, Typhoon Coming On), 1840, oil on canvas, 90.8 × 122.6 cm, Museum of Fine Arts, Boston. Photo: reproduced by courtesy of Museum of Fine Arts, Boston, Henry Lillie Pierce Fund, 99.22, © 2002.

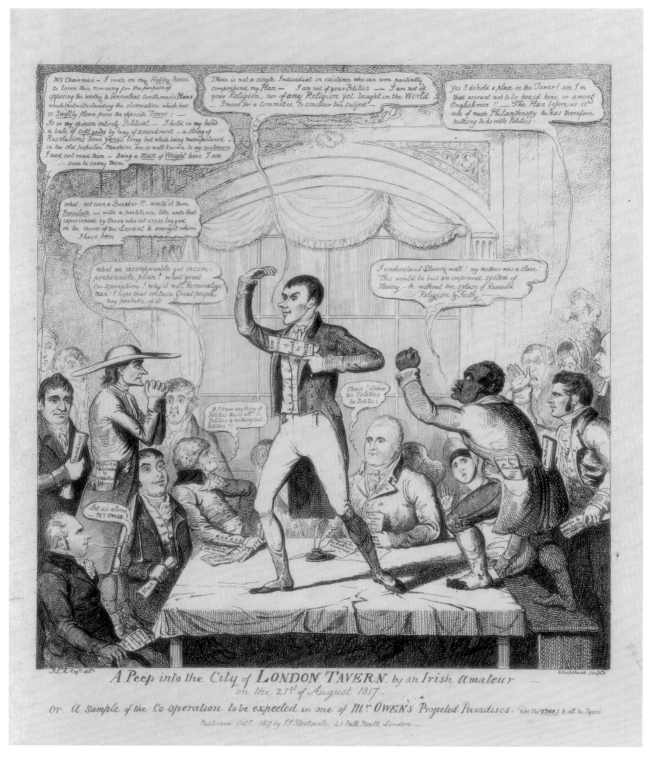

Plate 15.1   George Cruikshank, A Peep into the City of London Tavern by an Irish Amateur on 21 August 1817 – or A Sample of the Co-operation to be expected in one of Mr Owen's Projected Paradises *(Wedderburn arguing with Robert Owen), 1817, cartoon, published by J.J. Stockdale, British Museum, London.* Photo: *by courtesy of the Trustees of the British Museum.*

Plate 16.1 Joseph Wright of Derby, An Eruption of Mount Vesuvius, seen from Portici, c.1774–6, oil on canvas, 101.6 x 127 cm, University College of Wales, Aberystwyth. Photo: Bridgeman Art Library/John Webb.

Plate 16.2   John Robert Cozens, In the Canton of Unterwalden, *watercolour, 23.8 × 36.2 cm, Leeds Museums and Galleries (City Art Gallery). Photo: Bridgeman Art Library.*

Plate 16.3   Salvator Rosa, Landscape with Hermit, c.1662, *oil on canvas, 78.8 × 75.5 cm, Walker Art Gallery, Liverpool. Photo: courtesy of the Board of Trustees of the National Museums and Galleries on Merseyside (Walker Art Gallery), Liverpool.*

Plate 16.4 Salvator Rosa, Mercury, Argus and Io, c.1653–4, oil on canvas, 112.1 x 141.9 cm, Nelson–Atkins Museum of Art, Kansas City.
Photo: reproduced courtesy of The Nelson–Atkins Museum of Art, Kansas City, Missouri (Purchase: Nelson Trust, 32–192/1).

Plate 16.5   *Gaspard Dughet (called Gaspard Poussin),* The Falls of Tivoli, *oil on canvas, 100 × 83 cm, Wallace Collection, London. Photo: reproduced by permission of the Trustees of the Wallace Collection, London.*

Plate 16.6   Francis Nicholson, Lake Windermere, 18052, watercolour, 38.5 × 53.5 cm, Whitworth Art Gallery, Manchester. Photo: reproduced by kind permission of the Whitworth Art Gallery, University of Manchester.

64

Plate 16.7   Claude Lorrain, The Father of Psyche Sacrificing at the Temple of Apollo, 1662, oil on canvas, 175.5 × 223 cm. Anglesey Abbey, Lode, Cambs. Photo: Anglesey Abbey, The Fairhaven Collection (The National Trust), NTPL/John Hammond.

Plate 16.8   Jacob van Ruisdael, A Waterfall in a Rocky Landscape, *c.1660–70, oil on canvas, 98.5 × 85 cm, National Gallery, London. Photo: © The National Gallery, London.*

Plate 16.9   Thomas Gainsborough, Gainsborough's Forest (Cornard Wood), c.1748, oil on canvas, 121.9 x 154.9 cm, National Gallery, London. Photo: © The National Gallery, London.

Plate 16.10   Richard Wilson, Snowdon from Llyn Nantlle, c.1765, Walker Art Gallery, Liverpool. Photo: courtesy of the Board of Trustees of the National Museums and Galleries on Merseyside (Walker Art Gallery), Liverpool.

Plate 16.11   J.M.W. Turner, Thomson's Aeolian Harp, 1809, oil on canvas, 166.7 x 306 cm, Manchester Art Gallery. Photo: © Manchester Art Gallery.

Plate 17.1   John 'Warwick' Smith, Pocklington's Island, Keswick Lake *from* Twenty Views of the Lake District, *engraver J. Merigot, etching with aquatint, hand-coloured, 33 × 47 cm, British Library, London. Photo: reproduced by permission of the British Library, London (shelfmark 1899.t.3).*

Plate 17.2   Philip de Loutherbourg, Belle Isle, Windermere, in a Calm, *1786, oil on canvas, 135.9 × 209.6 cm, Abbot Hall Art Gallery, Kendal. Photo: Bridgeman Art Library.*

Plate 17.3   Joseph Wright of Derby, Derwentwater with Skiddaw in the Distance, *1795–6, oil on canvas, 56.5 x 78.7 cm, Yale Center for British Art, Paul Mellon Collection, New Haven. Photo: Bridgeman Art Library.*

Plate 17.4   J.M.W. Turner, Inside Tintern Abbey, Monmouthshire, c.1794, *pencil and watercolour, 32.1 x 25.1 cm, Victoria and Albert Museum, London. Photo: V&A Images, Victoria and Albert Museum, London.*

Plate 17.5 J.M.W. Turner, Derwentwater, Lodore Falls and Borrowdale from Headland beyond Calfclose Bay, *1797, watercolour, 49.3 × 62.9 cm, Tate Gallery, London. Photo: © Tate, London, 2002.*

Plate 17.6 Claude Lorrain, Landscape with a Procession to Delphi, *1650, oil on canvas, 150 × 200 cm, Galleria Doria Pamphili, Rome. Photo: Scala, Florence.*

Plate 17.7   J.M.W. Turner, Windermere, 1821, watercolour, 29.2 × 40.7 cm, Abbot Hall Art Gallery, Kendal. Photo: reproduced by kind permission of Abbot Hall Art Gallery, Kendal, Cumbria.

72

Plate 17.8   J.M.W. Turner, Crummock Water from Buttermere Hause, 1797, pencil and watercolour, 27.4 × 37 cm, Tate Gallery, London. Photo: © Tate, London, 2002.

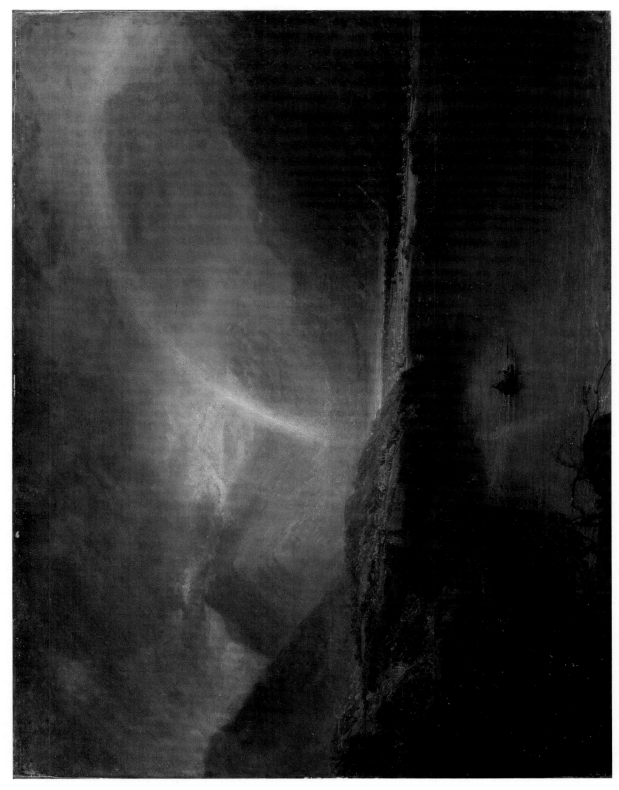

Plate 17.9   J.M.W. Turner, Buttermere Lake, with part of Cromackwater, Cumberland, a Shower, 1798, oil on canvas, 91.5 x 122 cm, Tate Gallery, London. Photo: © Tate, London, 2002.

Plate 17.10 Rembrandt van Rijn, The Stone Bridge, c.1638, oil on panel, 29.5 x 42.5 cm, Rijksmuseum, Amsterdam. Photo: reproduced by kind permission of Rijksmuseum, Amsterdam.

Plate 17.11   Peter Paul Rubens, The Rainbow Landscape, c.1636, oil on canvas, 137 x 237 cm, Wallace Collection, London. Photo: reproduced by kind permission of the trustees of the Wallace Collection, London.

Plate 17.12 J.M.W. Turner, The Old Mill, Ambleside, *watercolour, 36.8 x 25.4 cm, University of Liverpool Art Gallery &*
Collections. Photo: Bridgeman Art Library.

Plate 17.13   J.M.W. Turner, Morning amongst the Coniston Fells, Cumberland, *1798, oil on canvas, 123 × 89.7 cm, Tate Gallery, London. Photo: © Tate, London, 2002.*

Plate 17.14   John Constable, Dedham Vale, *September 1802, oil on canvas, 43.5 × 34.5 cm, Victoria and Albert Museum, London. Photo: V&A Images, Victoria and Albert Museum, London. (This is an early oil sketch for a finished work of 1828.)*

Plate 17.15 Claude Lorrain, Landscape with Hagar and the Angel, *1656, oil on canvas, 52.7 x 43.8 cm, National Gallery, London.* Photo: © *The National Gallery, London.*

Plate 17.16   Willie Lott's cottage, 2003, photograph, Ipswich Museum. Photo: Ipswich Borough Council Museums & Galleries.

Plate 17.17 John Constable, Gate Crag, Borrowdale, *1806, pencil and watercolour, 44.4 x 34.4 cm, Victoria and Albert Museum, London. Photo: V&A Images, Victoria and Albert Museum, London.*

Plate 17.18   John Constable, View in Borrowdale, October 1806, pencil and watercolour, 14 x 38 cm, Victoria and Albert Museum, London. Photo: V&A Images, Victoria and Albert Museum, London.

Plate 17.19   John Constable, Cloud Study with Horizon of Trees, *September 1821, oil on paper, laid on board, red ground, 25 x 29 cm, Royal Academy of Arts, London. Photo: © The Royal Academy of Arts, London.*

Plate 17.20   John Constable, Landscape and Double Rainbow, *1812, oil on paper, laid on canvas, 33.7 x 38.4 cm, Victoria and Albert Museum, London. Photo: V&A Images, Victoria and Albert Museum, London.*

Plate 17.21   John Constable, The Haywain, 1821, oil on canvas, 130.5 × 185.4 cm, National Gallery, London. Photo: © The National Gallery, London.

Plate 17.22 John Constable The Leaping Horse, 1824–5, oil on canvas, 142 × 187.3 cm, Royal Academy of Arts, London. Photo: © Royal Academy of Arts, London, 1992. Photographer: Prudence Cuming Associates.

Plate 17.23   John Constable, Stonehenge, *1836, watercolour, 38.5 × 59 cm, Victoria and Albert Museum, London. Photo: V&A Images, Victoria and Albert Museum, London.*

Plate 17.24   John Constable, The Sea near Brighton, *1826, oil on paper, laid on card, 17.5 × 23.8 cm, Tate Gallery, London. Photo: © Tate, London, 2002.*

Plate 17.25   J.M.W. Turner, Ullswater, looking south from Aria Point, *1797, pencil sketch, 27.4 x 37 cm, Tate Gallery, London. Photo: © Tate, London, 2002. (Some fading has occurred to this sketch over time.)*

Plate 17.26   J.M.W. Turner, Derwentwater from Friar's Crag, near Keswick, *1801, watercolour, 38.3 x 54.9 cm, Tate Gallery, London. Photo: © Tate, London, 2002.*

Plate 17.27   J.M.W. Turner, Lodore Falls, 1797, pencil and watercolour, 37 × 27.4 cm, Tate Gallery, London. Photo: © Tate, London, 2002.

Plate 17.28 J.M.W. Turner, Ullswater Lake from Gowbarrow Park, Cumberland, c.1815, watercolour, 28 x 41.3 cm, Whitworth Art Gallery, Manchester.

Photo: reproduced by kind permission of the Whitworth Art Gallery, University of Manchester.

Plate 17.29 J.M.W. Turner, The Fall of Clyde, Lanarkshire: Noon – Vide Akenside's Hymn to the Naiads, *1802, watercolour, Walker Art Gallery, Liverpool. Photo: courtesy of the Board of Trustees of the National Museums and Galleries on Merseyside (Walker Art Gallery), Liverpool.*

Plate 17.30 John Constable, Windermere, *1806, watercolour and pencil on paper, 20.2 × 37.8 cm, Fitzwilliam Museum, Cambridge. Photo: courtesy of Fitzwilliam Museum, Cambridge.*

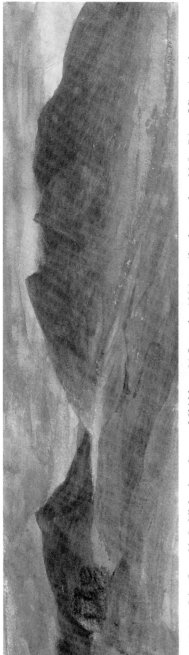

Plate 17.31 John Constable, Saddleback and part of Skiddaw, 21 September 1806, pencil and watercolour, 29.5 x 76 cm, Victoria and Albert Museum, London. Photo: V&A Images, Victoria and Albert Museum, London.

Plate 17.32 John Constable, Derwentwater: Stormy Evening, October 1806, pencil and watercolour, 10.4 x 23.9 cm, Victoria and Albert Museum, London. Photo: V&A Images, Victoria and Albert Museum, London.

Plate 17.33   John Constable, View in Langdale, *October 1806, pencil and grey wash, 34.4 × 48.6 cm, Victoria and Albert Museum, London. Photo: V&A Images, Victoria and Albert Museum, London.*

Plate 17.34 John Constable, Taylor Ghyll, Sty Head, Borrowdale, *September 1806, pencil with grey and pink wash, Victoria and Albert Museum, London. Photo: V&A Images, Victoria and Albert Museum, London.*

Plate 17.35   John Constable, Hadleigh Castle: The Mouth of the Thames, *1829, oil on canvas, 122 × 164.5 cm, Yale Center for British Art, Paul Mellon Collection, New Haven. Photo: Bridgeman Art Library.*

Plate 17.36   John Constable, Helvellyn, *watercolour sketch, Dove Cottage, Grasmere. Photo: courtesy of Dove Cottage, The Wordsworth Trust.*

Plate 17.37   Claude Lorrain, Landscape with Cephalus and Procris reunited by Diana, 1645, oil on canvas, 101.6 × 132.1 cm, National Gallery, London. Photo: © The National Gallery, London.

Plate 17.38 Jacob van Ruisdael, Two Watermills and an Open Sluice at Singraven, early 1650s, oil on canvas, 87.3 x 111.5 cm, National Gallery, London. Photo: © The National Gallery, London.

Plate 17.39   Richard Wilson, Solitude, 1762, oil on canvas, 101 x 125 cm, Glynn Vivian Art Gallery, Swansea.

Plate 17.40   Thomas Hearne, Sir George
Beaumont and Joseph Farington sketching
a Waterfall, *c.1777, watercolour, 44.5 x 29.2
cm, Dove Cottage, Grasmere. Photo: courtesy of
Dove Cottage, The Wordsworth Trust.*

Plate 17.41   Thomas Hearne,
Sir George Beaumont and
Joseph Farington sketching in
Oils, *c.1777, pencil sketch,
17.8 x 19.1 cm, Dove Cottage,
Grasmere. Photo: courtesy of Dove
Cottage, The Wordsworth Trust.*

Plate 17.42   Thomas Hearne, Derwentwater from Skiddaw, *pencil and watercolour on paper, 18.8 x 27 cm, Leeds Museums and Galleries (City Art Gallery) UK. Photo: Bridgeman Art Library.*

Plate 17.43   Edward Dayes, Keswick Lake and Skiddaw, c.1791, *pen, blue and grey wash, Dove Cottage, Grasmere. Photo: courtesy of Dove Cottage, The Wordsworth Trust.*

Plate 17.44   Joseph Wilkinson, Part of Newlands Vale, 1795, watercolour, Dove Cottage, Grasmere. Photo: courtesy of Dove Cottage, The Wordsworth Trust.

Plate 17.45   Paul Sandby, Keswick Lake, 1793, watercolour, 36.8 × 54.6 cm, Aberdeen Art Gallery and Museums.

Plate 17.46   Joseph Wright of Derby, Ullswater, c.1794–5, oil on canvas, Dove Cottage, Grasmere. Photo: courtesy of Dove Cottage, The Wordsworth Trust.

Plate 17.47   Francis Towne, Keswick Lake looking towards Lodore Falls, 1805, watercolour, private collection. Photo: © Christie's Images Ltd, 2004.

Plate 17.48   Thomas Girtin, The Falls of the Ogwen, North Wales, *c. 1799, watercolour, 53.6 x 44.5 cm, Ashmolean Museum, Oxford. Photo: courtesy of the Ashmolean Museum, Oxford.*

Plate 17.49   William Havell, Windermere, 1811?, watercolour, 24.8 × 34 cm, British Museum, London. Photo: © British Museum.

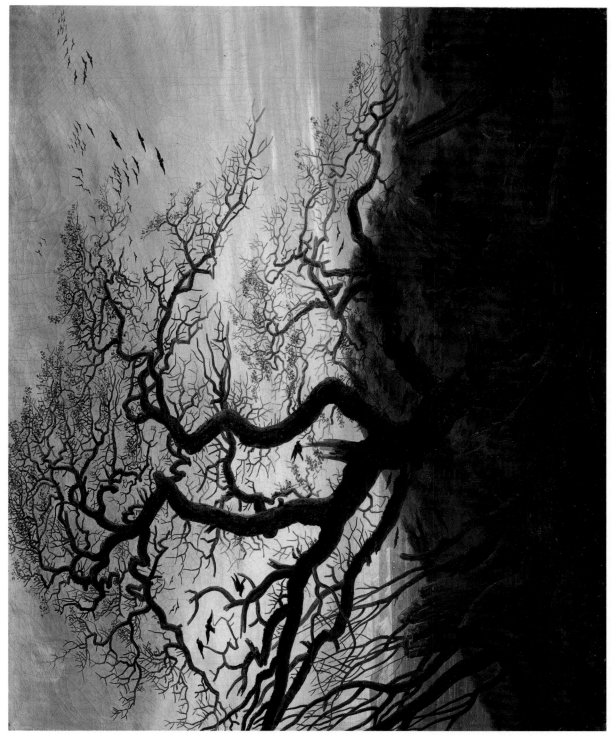

Plate 17.50   Caspar David Friedrich, Tree with Crows, 1822, oil on canvas, 54 × 71 cm, Louvre, Paris. Photo: © RMN/Arnaudet.

Plate 18.1   J.M.W. Turner, The Falls of Clyde, c.1844–6, oil on canvas, 89 × 119.5 cm, Lady Lever Art Gallery, Port Sunlight. Photo: reproduced by kind permission of Board of Trustees of the National Museums and Galleries on Merseyside.

Plate 18.2 G. Hunt, Dancing Class, The Institute, New Lanark, c.1820, coloured engraving, New Lanark Conservation Trust. Photo: reproduced by kind permission of New Lanark Conservation Trust.

This shows a schoolroom scene in the Institute for the Formation of Character, with the dancing children and famous visual aids. The aids were the work of Catherine Whitwell, sister of the Owenite architect Stedman Whitwell and allegedly an advocate of free love.

Plate 20.1 Joseph Wright of Derby, An Experiment on a Bird in the Air Pump, 1768, oil on canvas, 182.9 x 243.9 cm, National Gallery, London. Photo: © The National Gallery, London.

A reproduction which enables you to see details of the room more clearly can be found on the National Gallery's website: http://www.nationalgallery.org.uk. Go to 'Collection', then 'Explore the collection online'. Use the 'Full Collection Index' to find the painting.

*Plate 20.2   Alexandre-Evariste Fragonard, Volta before the First Consul, Napoleon examining Volta's Pile, 1810 or c.1830, oil on canvas.
Photo: © RMN/Bulloz Collection.*

In addition to a Voltaic pile, the apparatus on the table includes, to its right, Leyden jars, which were devices for demonstrating static electricity; and, to its left, apparatus for the electrolysis of water. In this representation, it is unclear that anything is being actively demonstrated since the apparatus seems merely to be placed on a table in a salon rather than in a working environment.

Plate 20.3   James Gillray, Scientific Researches – New Discoveries in Pneumaticks! – or – an Experimental Lecture on the Powers of Air, 1802, coloured etching, 24.8 x 35 cm, Royal Institution, London. Photo: Bridgeman Art Library.

Plate 20.4   Henry Howard, Sir Humphry Davy, *1803, oil on canvas, 128.3 × 102.9 cm, National Portrait Gallery, London.*

112

Plate 20.5   George Garrard, Sheep Shearing at Woburn, 1804, oil on canvas, Woburn Abbey. Photo: reproduced by kind permission of The Marquess of Tavistock and the Trustees of the Bedford Estates; © Marquess of Tavistock and the Trustees of the Bedford Estates.

Whetstone Park

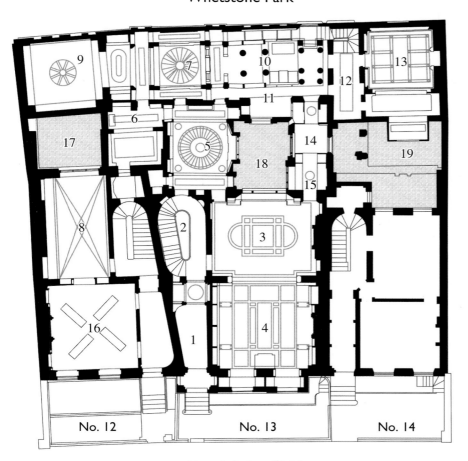

No. 12 **No. 13** **No. 14**

Lincoln's Inn Fields

Legend

1 Entrance Hall

2 Staircase

3 Dining Room

4 Library

5 Breakfast Parlour

6 Anteroom

7 Dome

8 Breakfast Parlour No. 12

9 New Picture Room

10 Colonnade

11 South Passage

12 Corridor

13 Picture Room

14 Dressing Room

15 Study

16 Dining Room No. 12
(now exhibition space)

17 New Court

18 Monument Court

19 Monk's Yard

Plate 22.1   Ground-floor plan of Sir John Soane's Museum today, from A New Description of Sir John Soane's Museum, *Libanus Press, 2001, p.ix. Photo: by courtesy of the Trustees of the Soane Museum, London.*

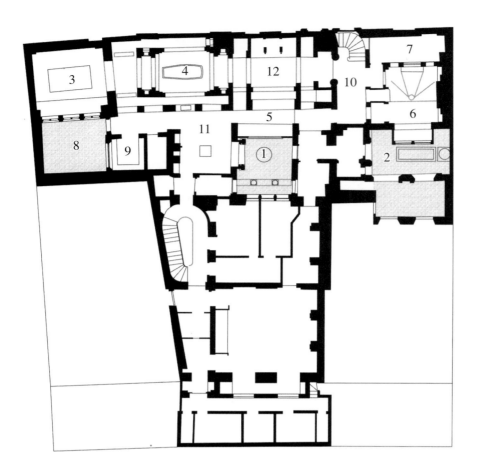

Legend

1 Monument Court

2 Monk's Yard

3 West Chamber

4 Sepulchral Chamber

5 Flaxman Recess

6 Monk's Parlour

7 Monk's Cell

8 New Court

9 Catacombs (Columbarium)

10 Basement Stairwell

11 Basement Anteroom

12 Egyptian Crypt

Plate 22.2   Basement-floor plan of Sir John Soane's Museum today, from A New Description of Sir John Soane's Museum, *Libanus Press, 2001, p.x. Photo: by courtesy of the Trustees of the Soane Museum, London.*

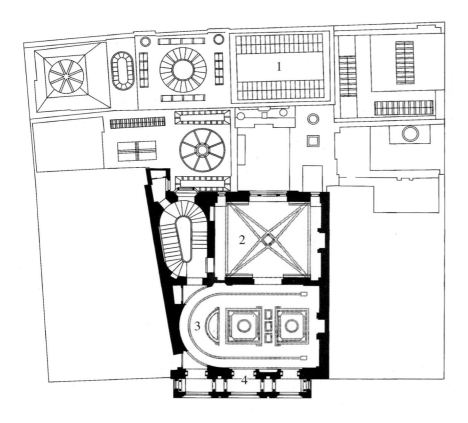

Legend

1 Upper Drawing Office
   (Note: the plan shows the skylights over the Upper Drawing Office.)

2 North Drawing Room

3 South Drawing Room

4 Loggia

Plate 22.3   First-floor plan of Sir John Soane's Museum today, from A New Description of Sir John Soane's Museum, *Libanus Press, 2001, p.xi. Photo: by courtesy of the Trustees of the Soane Museum, London.*

Plate 22.4   George Dance Jr, All Hallows Church Interior, Royal Academy lecture drawing, 1816, pen, pencil and coloured washes, shaded, 98 × 72.5 cm, Sir John Soane's Museum, London. Photo: by courtesy of the Trustees of Sir John Soane's Museum, London. (SM 18/7/7)

Plate 22.5   Sir John Soane, The Elevation to the River of a Design for a Triumphal Bridge, *1777, pencil, pen and watercolour, 54.5 × 241 cm, Sir John Soane's Museum, London. Photo: by courtesy of the Trustees of Sir John Soane's Museum, London. (SM 12/5/4)*

Plate 22.6   View of Interior of Saint-Geneviève (Panthéon), Paris, Royal Academy lecture drawing, 1820, pencil, pen and watercolour, 111.2 × 72.4 cm, Sir John Soane's Museum, London. Photo: by courtesy of the Trustees of Sir John Soane's Museum, London. (SM 22/5/11)

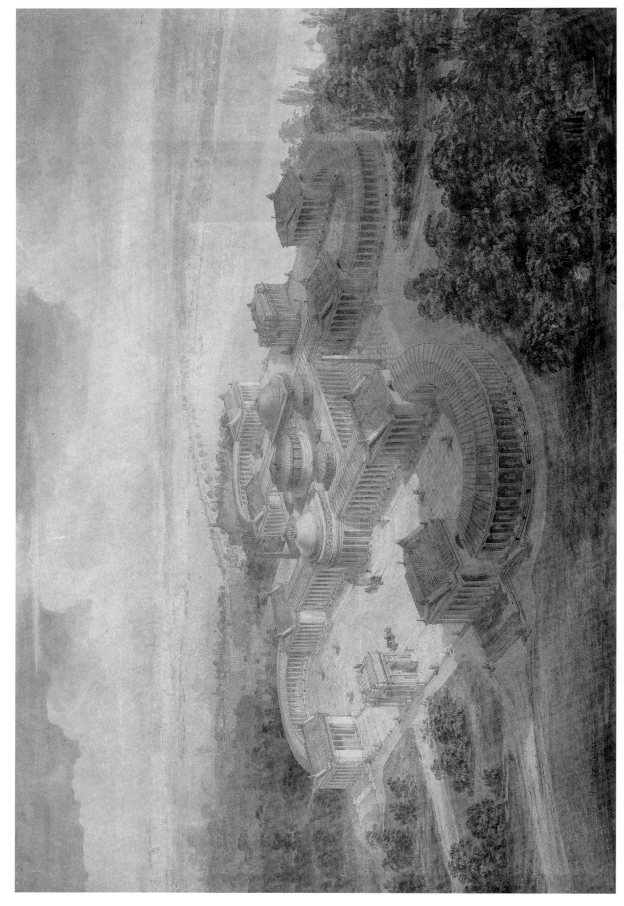

Plate 22.7   Sir John Soane, Design for a British Senate House, 1778, watercolour, Sir John Soane's Museum, London. Photo: by courtesy of the Trustees of Sir John Soane's Museum, London. (SM P254)

Plate 22.8 Tommaso Napoli, interior of *Villa Palagonia, Bagheria, near Palermo, Sicily,* c.1705. Photo: Tim Benton.

120

Plate 22.9   Sir John Soane, Design for House of Lords River Front, 1794, pen and ink washes, Sir John Soane's Museum, London.
Photo: by courtesy of the Trustees of Sir John Soane's Museum, London. (SM P273)

Plate 22.10   Joseph Michael Gandy, Design for Pitzhanger Manor Library, *1802, pen and watercolour, 96 × 129.5 cm, Sir John Soane's Museum, London. Photo: by courtesy of the Trustees of Sir John Soane's Museum, London. (SM P94)*

Plate 22.11   Henry Parke, Student measuring the Corinthian Order of the Temple of Jupiter Stator (Castor and Pollux), Rome, *Royal Academy lecture drawing, c.1807, pencil, pen and watercolour, 94. × 63.4 cm, Sir John Soane's Museum, London. Photo: by courtesy of the Trustees of Sir John Soane's Museum, London. (SM 23/9/3)*

Plate 22.12 Primitive Hut according to Vitruvius, *with figures of primitive tribesmen added by Antonio van Assen,*
Royal Academy lecture drawing, 1807, watercolour, 48.6 × 69 cm, Sir John Soane's Museum, London. Photo: by courtesy of
the Trustees of Sir John Soane's Museum, London. (SM 27/2/4)

Plate 22.13 The Origin of the Entablature of the Doric Order according to Vitruvius, *Royal Academy lecture*
drawing, c.1809–10, pen and watercolour, 61 × 88.8 cm, Sir John Soane's Museum, London. Photo: by courtesy of the
Trustees of Sir John Soane's Museum, London. (SM 23/4/8)

Plate 22.14 Royal Opera House, Covent Garden, London by Robert Smirke, *Royal Academy lecture drawing, 1809, pencil, pen, ink and watercolour, 57.4 × 94 cm, Sir John Soane's Museum, London. Photo: by courtesy of the Trustees of Sir John Soane's Museum, London. (SM 18/9/1)*

Plate 22.15   Joseph Michael Gandy, Scala Regia, Palace of Westminster, House of Lords, *1800, watercolour, 105 × 83 cm, Sir John Soane's Museum, London. Photo: by courtesy of the Trustees of Sir John Soane's Museum, London. (SM P283)*

Plate 22.16   Joseph Michael Gandy, Interior of Privy
Council Chamber, 1827, watercolour, 95.1 x 72.3 cm,
Sir John Soane's Museum, London. Photo: by courtesy
of the Trustees of Sir John Soane's Museum, London.
(SM 15/5/1)

Plate 22.17   George Underwood, Design for the Ark
of the Masonic Covenant, 1813–14, pen and coloured
washes, 122.8 x 79.5 cm, Sir John Soane's Museum,
London. Photo: by courtesy of the Trustees of Sir John
Soane's Museum, London. (SM 14/4/6)

Plate 22.18 Joseph Michael Gandy, View of Freemasons' Hall by Day, 1828, pen and watercolour, 93 × 130 cm, Sir John Soane's Museum, London. Photo: by courtesy of the Trustees of Sir John Soane's Museum, London. (SM P89)

127

Plate 22.19 Joseph Michael Gandy, Public and Private Buildings executed by Sir John Soane between 1780 and 1815, 1818, pencil, pen and ink, watercolour and bodycolour, 72.5 x 129.3 cm, Sir John Soane's Museum, London. Photo: by courtesy of the Trustees of Sir John Soane's Museum, London. (SM P87)

Plate 22.20   Joseph Michael Gandy, Architectural Visions of Early Fancy, 1820, pencil, pen and ink, watercolour and bodycolour, 73.5 × 130.5 cm, Sir John Soane's Museum, London. Photo: by courtesy of the Trustees of Sir John Soane's Museum, London. (SM P81)

Plate 22.21   Giovanni Altieri, Model of the Temple of Vesta at Tivoli, near Rome, *1770s, cork, 39.5 x 52.3 x 51.5 cm, Sir John Soane's Museum, London. Photo: by courtesy of the Trustees of Sir John Soane's Museum, London. (SM MR2)*

Plate 22.22   Sir John Soane, Bank of England, view of Lothbury Wall façade with Tivoli corner on the right, 1807, pen and watercolour, 31.9 × 91.7 cm, Sir John Soane's Museum, London. Photo: by courtesy of the Trustees of Sir John Soane's Museum, London. (SM 12/1/7)

Plate 22.23   Joseph Michael Gandy, View of Dome Area towards South-east, 12–13 Lincoln's Inn Fields, *1811, pen and watercolour, 119 × 88 cm, Sir John Soane's Museum, London. Photo: by courtesy of the Trustees of Sir John Soane's Museum, London. (SM 14/6/5)*

Plate 22.24   Joseph Michael Gandy, View of Museum towards East, 12–13 Lincoln's Inn Fields,
*1811, watercolour, 137 x 80 cm, Sir John Soane's Museum, London. Photo: by courtesy of the Trustees of
Sir John Soane's Museum, London. (SM P384)*

Plate 22.25 The 'Pasticcio' in the Monument Court, 13 Lincoln's Inn Fields, *erected 1819, drawn 19 August 1825, watercolour, Sir John Soane's Museum, London. Photo: by courtesy of the Trustees of Sir John Soane's Museum, London. (SM Vol 82/72)*

Plate 22.26   Joseph Michael Gandy, 'Sunset' View of Tyringham, 1798, pen and watercolour, 62.5 × 94.9 cm, Sir John Soane's Museum, London. Photo: by courtesy of the Trustees of Sir John Soane's Museum, London. (SM13/5/3)

Plate 22.27   Sir John Soane, Gateway, Tyringham, *detail. Photo: June Buck/ Country Life Picture Library, London.*

Plate 22.28   Joseph Michael Gandy, Design Perspective of the Interior of the Hall, with Inset Plans of the Hall and Chamber Floor, Tyringham, *1798, pen, ink and watercolour, 85 × 55.8 cm, Sir John Soane's Museum, London. Photo: by courtesy of the Trustees of Sir John Soane's Museum, London (SM 13/5/5)*

136

Plate 22.29 Joseph Michael Gandy, Preliminary Design for Lothbury Court, Bank of England, *with figures added by Antonio van Assen, 1798–9, pen and watercolour, 64.6 x 95.2 cm, Sir John Soane's Museum, London. Photo: by courtesy of the Trustees of Sir John Soane's Museum, London. (SM 12/3/13)*

Plate 22.30   Sir John Soane, Front Elevation Design, Pitzhanger Manor, 1800, pencil, pen, ink and watercolour, 53.1 × 72 cm, Sir John Soane's Museum, London.

Photo: by courtesy of the Trustees of Sir John Soane's Museum, London. (SM 31/2/47)

138

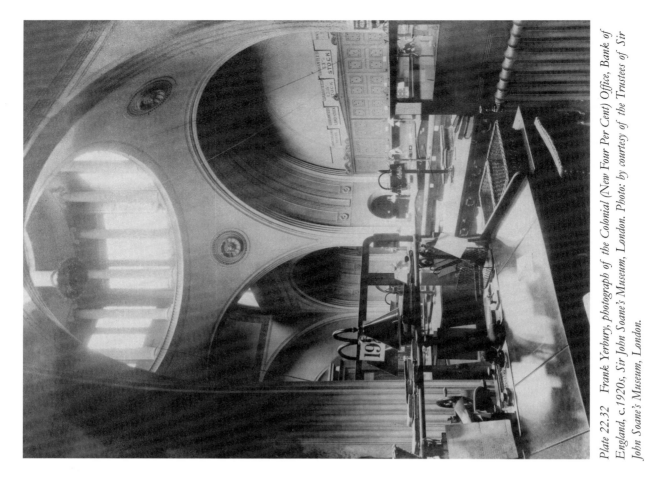

Plate 22.32   Frank Yerbury, photograph of the Colonial (New Four Per Cent) Office, Bank of England, c.1920s, Sir John Soane's Museum, London. Photo: by courtesy of the Trustees of Sir John Soane's Museum, London.

Plate 22.31   Frank Yerbury, photograph of the Old Dividend (Old Four Per Cent) Office, Bank of England, c.1920s, Sir John Soane's Museum, London. Photo: by courtesy of the Trustees of Sir John Soane's Museum, London.

Plate 22.33   Joseph Michael Gandy, View of Breakfast Parlour, 12 Lincoln's Inn Fields, *1798, watercolour, 64.5 × 65 cm, Sir John Soane's Museum, London. Photo: by courtesy of the Trustees of Sir John Soane's Museum, London. (SM 14/6/1)*

140

Plate 22.34   Charles-Louis Clérisseau, Interior of a Sepulchral Chamber, 1773, bodycolour, 46.9 × 60 cm, Sir John Soane's Museum, London. Photo: by courtesy of the Trustees of Sir John Soane's Museum, London. (SM P97)

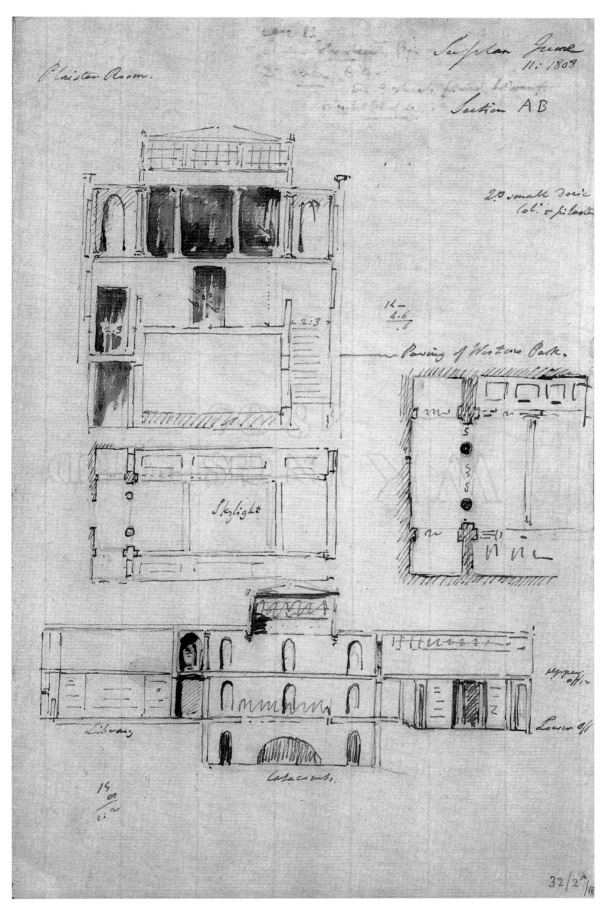

Plate 22.35   Sir John Soane, Designs for 'Plaister Room' or Museum at the Rear of *12–13 Lincoln's Inn Fields, 1808, pen and ink, 32.2 x 20 cm, Sir John Soane's Museum, London. Photo: by courtesy of the Trustees of Sir John Soane's Museum, London. (SM 32/2A/1A)*

Plate 22.36   Frank Copland, Sectional View of Dome and Breakfast Parlour, 13 Lincoln's Inn Fields, 1818, pen and watercolour, 54.5 x 64.0 cm, Sir John Soane's Museum, London. Photo: by courtesy of the Trustees of Sir John Soane's Museum, London. (SM Vol 83/1)

Plate 22.37   Joseph Michael Gandy, Front Elevation of 13 Lincoln's Inn Fields, *1812, watercolour,*
78 x 44.5 cm, Sir John Soane's Museum, London. Photo: by courtesy of the Trustees of Sir John Soane's
Museum, London/Ole Woldbye. (SM 14/6/2)

Plate 22.38   Ephesian Artemis or Diana, *Roman antique, black marble head (hands and feet restored), Sir John Soane's Museum, London. Photo: by courtesy of the Trustees of Sir John Soane's Museum, London/Ole Woldbye. (SM M612)*

Plate 22.39   George Basevi, Sectional View of Museum towards North, 12–13 Lincoln's Inn Fields, *1812, pencil, pen, ink and watercolour, 125.2 x 74.1 cm, Sir John Soane's Museum, London. Photo: by courtesy of the Trustees of Sir John Soane's Museum, London. (SM 14/6/7)*

Plate 22.40   Joseph Michael Gandy, Soane Funerary Monument, 1816, watercolour, 66.5 x 97 cm, Sir John Soane's Museum, London. Photo: by courtesy of the Trustees of Sir John Soane's Museum, London. (SM 14/4/8)

Plate 22.41   Joseph Michael Gandy, Composite View of Museum: Detail of South Passage of Colonnade, looking West, *1822, Sir John Soane's Museum, London. Photo: by courtesy of the Trustees of Sir John Soane's Museum, London. Photo: A.C. Cooper. (SM P113)*

Plate 22.42   *Joseph Michael Gandy,* View into Monk's Parlour to East, 14 Lincoln's Inn Fields, *1825, watercolour, Sir John Soane's Museum, London. Photo: by courtesy of the Trustees of Sir John Soane's Museum, London. (SM Vol 82/67)*

Plate 22.43   Joseph Michael Gandy, Design for Pitzhanger Manor Breakfast Room, 1802, watercolour, 97 × 129.5 cm, Sir John Soane's Museum, London. Photo: by courtesy of the Trustees of Sir John Soane's Museum, London. (SM P95)

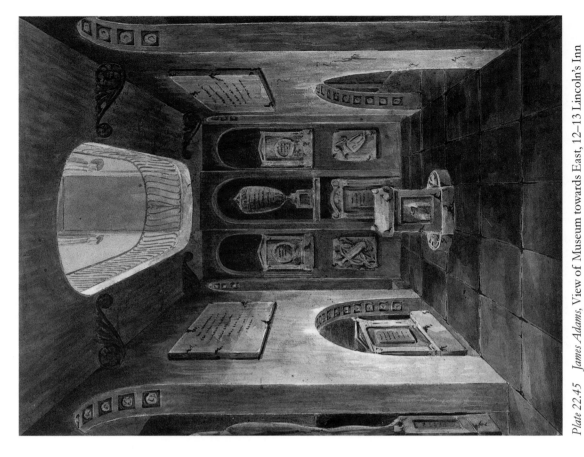

Plate 22.45   James Adams, View of Museum towards East, 12–13 Lincoln's Inn Fields, Basement, 1808, pencil, pen, ink and watercolour, 52 x 43.5 cm, Sir John Soane's Museum, London. Photo: by courtesy of the Trustees of Sir John Soane's Museum, London. (SM Vol 83/35)

Plate 22.44   James Adams, View of Museum towards East, 12–13 Lincoln's Inn Fields, 1808, pencil, pen, ink and watercolour, 48.5 x 44.6 cm, Sir John Soane's Museum, London. Photo: by courtesy of the Trustees of Sir John Soane's Museum, London. (SM Vol 83/34)

Plate 22.46   *George Bailey*, Sectional View of Dome towards East, 12–13 Lincoln's Inn Fields, *1811, watercolour, 96 × 62.5 cm, Sir John Soane's Museum, London. Photo: by courtesy of the Trustees of Sir John Soane's Museum, London. (SM 14/6/3)*

Plate 22.47   James Adams, Design for the Museum: Sectional Perspective Design for the Museum, looking East, 12–13 Lincoln's Inn Fields, *29 July 1808, Sir John Soane's Museum, London. Photo: by courtesy of the Trustees of Sir John Soane's Museum, London. (SM 83/36)*

Plate 22.48 Section of North Elevation of Dome, with Columnar Arrangement, 12–13 Lincoln's Inn Fields, *1808, Sir John Soane's Museum, London. Photo: by courtesy of the Trustees of Sir John Soane's Museum, London. (SM 32/3/37)*

Plate 24.1   Joshua Reynolds, Theory, *1779, oil on canvas, 172.7 × 172.7 cm, Royal Academy of Arts, London. Photo: reproduced by kind permission of Royal Academy of Arts, London.*

Plate 24.2   *Caspar David Friedrich, Monk by the Sea, 1809–10, oil on canvas, 110 x 171.5 cm, National Gallery, Berlin. © BPK, Berlin. Photo: Jörg P. Anders, Berlin/Jahr, 1993.*

Plate 28.1   *Moritz von Schwind*, An Evening at Josef von Spaun's: Schubert at the Piano with the Operatic Baritone Johann Michael Vogl, *1868, sepia drawing, Historisches Museum der Stadt Wein. Photo: Bridgeman Art Library.*

Plate 28.2   *Leopold Kupelwieser,* The Family of Franz von Schober playing Charades, *1821, watercolour, Historisches Museum der Stadt Wein. Photo: Bridgeman Art Library.*

Heidenröslein.

Gedicht von J. W. v. Goethe.

Für eine Singstimme mit Begleitung des Pianoforte

componirt von

Schubert's Werke.

N.º 114.

FRANZ SCHUBERT.

Op. 3. N.º 3.

Ignaz Edlen von Mosel gewidmet.

19. August 1815.

Plate 28.3   Franz Schubert, score of Heidenröslein, *from* Franz Schubert: Lieder and Songs for One Voice, *Kalmus Study Scores No. 1074, Edwin F. Kalmus, New York (facsimile edition of* Franz Schuberts Werke: Kritisch durchgesehene Gesamtausgabe, *ed. E. Mandyczewski, J. Brahms and others, Leipzig, 1884–97).*

Plate 28.4 *Franz Schubert, score of* Gretchen am Spinnrade, *from* Franz Schubert: Lieder and Songs for One Voice, *Kalmus Study Scores No. 1070, Edwin F. Kalmus, New York (facsimile edition of* Franz Schuberts Werke: Kritisch durchgesehene Gesamtausgabe, *ed. E. Mandyczewski, J. Brahms and others, Leipzig, 1884–97).*

fin - de sie nim - mer und nim - - mer mehr.

Nach ihm _____ nur schau' ich zum

Fen - - ster hin - aus, nach ihm _____ nur geh' ich

aus _____ dem Haus. Sein ho - - her Gang, _____ sein'

ed' - - le Ge - stalt, sei - nes Mun - - des Lä - cheln, sei - ner

Au - - gen Ge - walt, und sei - - ner Re - de

Zau - - ber fluss, sein Hän - de druck,

und ach, sein Kuss!

Mei - ne Ruh' _____ ist hin, mein

Herz _____ ist schwer, _____ ich fin - de, ich fin - de sie

nim _ mer und nim _ _ mer _ mehr.

Mein Bu _ _ sen drängt sich nach _ _ _ ihm

p   *cresc. poco a poco*

hin,   ach dürft' _ _ _ _ ich fas _ sen und hal _ _ ten

accel.

f

ihn,   und küs _ _ _ sen ihn, _ _ _ _ so wie _ _ _ _ ich

ff

wollt;   an sei _ _ nen Küs _ sen ver _ ge _ _ hen

Erlkönig.

Ballade von J. W. v. Goethe.

Für eine Singstimme mit Begleitung des Pianoforte

componirt von

FRANZ SCHUBERT.

Vierte, endgiltige Fassung.

Op. 1.

Moriz Grafen von Dietrichstein gewidmet.

Schubert's Werke.

N<u>o</u> 178<u>d</u>

Plate 28.5 Franz Schubert, score of Erlkönig, *from* Franz Schubert: Lieder and Songs for One Voice, *Kalmus Study Scores No. 1076, Edwin F. Kalmus, New York (facsimile edition of* Franz Schuberts Werke: Kritisch durchgesehene Gesamtausgabe, *ed. E. Mandyczewski, J. Brahms and others, Leipzig, 1884–97).*

Erlkönig.

Ballade von J. W. v. Goethe.

Für eine Singstimme mit Begleitung des Pianoforte

Schubert's Werke. componirt von N.º 178ᵈ

FRANZ SCHUBERT.

Vierte, endgiltige Fassung.

Op. 1.

Moriz Grafen von Dietrichstein gewidmet.

Plate 28.5   Franz Schubert, score of Erlkönig, *from* Franz Schubert: Lieder and Songs for One Voice, *Kalmus Study Scores No. 1076, Edwin F. Kalmus, New York (facsimile edition of* Franz Schuberts Werke: Kritisch durchgesehene Gesamtausgabe, *ed. E. Mandyczewski, J. Brahms and others, Leipzig, 1884–97).*

Du kühl'st den bren - nenden Durst

mei - nes Busens, lieb - li - cher Mor - gen - wind!

p

decresc.

Ruft drein die Nach - ti - gall lie - bend nach mir aus dem

Ne - bel - thal.

dimin.

Plate 29.1 Alexandre Calame, View of Geneva, taken from Villa Diodati, formerly the home of Lord Byron, 1816, lithograph, Centre d'iconographie, Geneva.
Photo: Bibliothèque publique et Universitaire, collection iconographique, Genève.

176

Plate 29.2   David Wilkie, Chelsea Pensioners reading the Waterloo Despatch, 1822, Victoria and Albert Museum, London. Photo: V&A Images, Victoria and Albert Museum, London.

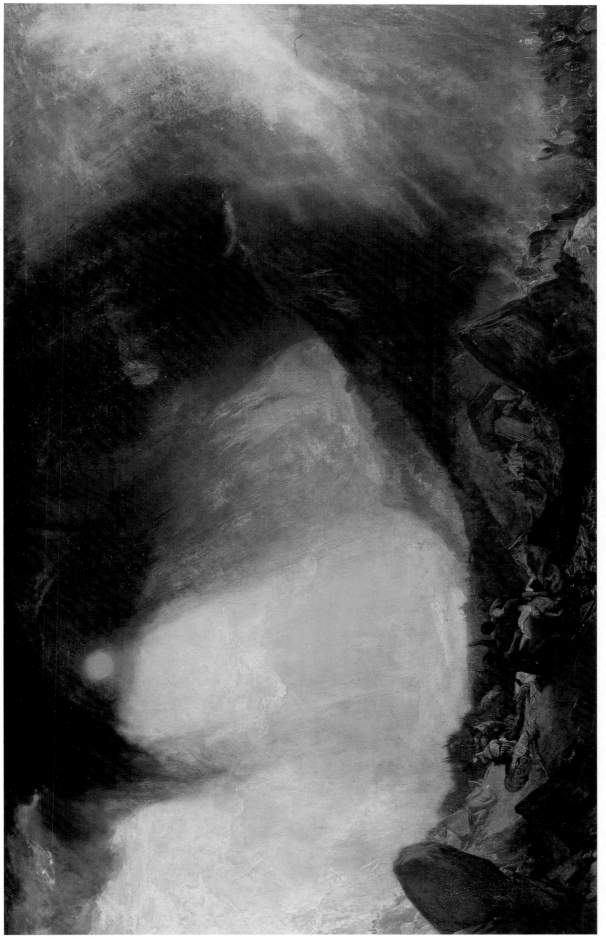

Plate 29.3   J.M.W. Turner, Snow Storm: Hannibal and his Army crossing the Alps, 1812, oil on canvas, 146 × 237.5 cm, Tate Gallery, London. Photo: © Tate, London, 2002.

Plate 29.4   J.M.W. Turner, The Field of Waterloo, *oil on canvas, 1818, 147.3 × 238.8 cm, Tate Gallery, London. Photo: © Tate, London, 2003.*

Plate 29.5 George Sanders, George Gordon, Sixth Lord Byron, *1807–8, oil on canvas, Royal Collection. Photo: The Royal Collection © 2003, Her Majesty Queen Elizabeth II.*

Plate 29.6   Richard Westall, Byron at the Age of 25, *1813, oil on canvas, 91.4 x 71.1 cm, National Portrait Gallery, London. Photo: courtesy of the National Portrait Gallery, London.*

Plate 29.7 Thomas Phillips, George Gordon Byron, 6th Baron, *1814. Photo: © Queen's Printer and Controller of HMSO, 2002,* UK Government Art Collection.

Plate 31.1   The west front of the Royal Pavilion, Brighton, from John Nash's Views of the Royal Pavilion, Brighton, 1826, aquatint. Photo: RIBA Library Photographs Collection.

183

Plate 31.2   The east front of the Royal Pavilion, Brighton, from John Nash's Views of the Royal Pavilion, Brighton, 1826, aquatint. Photo: RIBA Library Photographs Collection.

Plate 31.3   The Octagon Hall *(designed by Frederick Grace), from John Nash's Views of the Royal Pavilion, Brighton, 1826, aquatint.*
Photo: RIBA Library Photographs Collection.

Plate 31.4 The Entrance Hall *(designed by Frederick Grace), from John Nash's Views of the Royal Pavilion, Brighton, 1826, aquatint. Photo: RIBA Library Photographs Collection.*

Plate 31.5 The Long Gallery (designed by Frederick Crace), c.1815, from John Nash's Views of the Royal Pavilion, Brighton, 1826, aquatint.
Photo: RIBA Library Photographs Collection.

Plate 31.6   The Saloon (designed by Frederick Crace), 1815, from John Nash's Views of the Royal Pavilion, Brighton, 1826, aquatint.
Photo: RIBA Library Photographs Collection.

Plate 31.7   The Banqueting Room Gallery *(designed by Frederick Crace), c.1821, from John Nash's Views of the Royal Pavilion, Brighton, 1826, aquatint.*
Photo: RIBA Library Photographs Collection.

Plate 31.8 The Banqueting Room *(designed by Robert Jones), from John Nash's* Views of the Royal Pavilion, Brighton, *1826, aquatint. Photo: RIBA Library Photographs Collection.*

190

*Plate 31.9   The Saloon (designed by Robert Jones), 1825, from John Nash's Views of the Royal Pavilion, Brighton, 1826, aquatint.
Photo: RIBA Library Photographs Collection.*

Plate 31.10　The Music Room Gallery (designed by Frederick Crace), c.1821, from John Nash's Views of the Royal Pavilion, Brighton, 1826, aquatint.
Photo: RIBA Library Photographs Collection.

Plate 31.11   The Music Room (designed by Frederick Crace), from John Nash's Views of the Royal Pavilion, Brighton, 1826, aquatint.
Photo: RIBA Library Photographs Collection.

Plate 31.12   Jacob Spornberg, The Pavilion and the Steine, *1796. Photo: courtesy of the Royal Pavilion, Libraries and Museums, Brighton and Hove.*

Plate 31.13   Thomas Rowlandson, The Saloon, Marine Pavilion, *c.1789, watercolour, 22 x 29.4 cm. Photo: courtesy of the Royal Pavilion, Libraries and Museums, Brighton and Hove.*

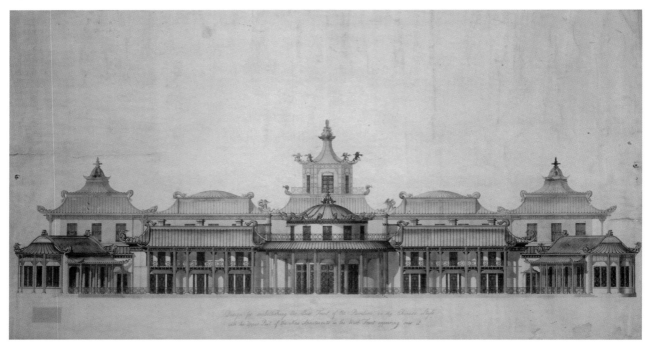

Plate 31.14   *William Porden*, Design for a Proposed Chinese Exterior, *1805, watercolour. Photo: courtesy of the Royal Pavilion, Libraries and Museums, Brighton and Hove.*

Plate 31.15   *Thomas Daniell*, The Jami' Masjid, Delhi, *plate XXIII from T. and W. Daniell,* Oriental Scenery, *1797, coloured aquatint, private collection. Photo: The Stapleton Collection/Bridgeman Art Library.*

Plate 31.16   Façade of Sezincote, 2003, photograph. Photo: Nicola Watson.

Plate 31.18 'Serpent Fountain', Sezincote, 2003, photograph. Photo: Nicola Watson.

Plate 31.17 Façade of Sezincote, detail, 2003, photograph. Photo: Nicola Watson.

Plate 31.19   Lacock Abbey, Wiltshire. Photo: reproduced by kind permission of Provincial Pictures, Bath. Photographer: Philip Pierce.

198

Plate 31.20 Cross-section of the Royal Pavilion, *from John Nash's Views of the Royal Pavilion, Brighton, 1826, aquatint. Photo: RIBA Library Photographs Collection.*

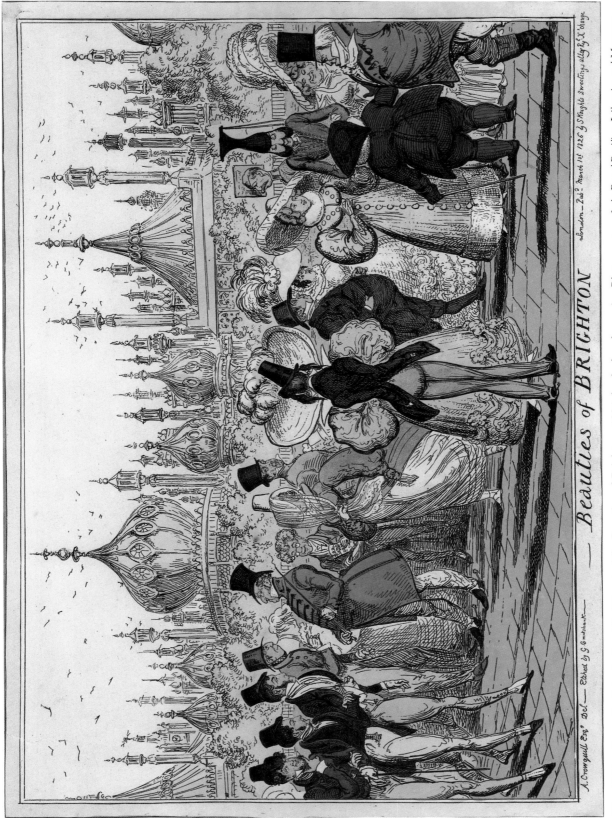

— Beauties of BRIGHTON —

A. Crowquill Esq.ʳ Del — Etched by G G Cruikshank.— London. Pub.ᵈ March 1st 1826 by S Knight sweeting's alley R.ˡ X change

Plate 31.21   George Cruikshank after Alfred Forrester, The Beauties of Brighton, 1826, hand-coloured engraving. Photo: courtesy of the Royal Pavilion, Libraries and Museums, Brighton and Hove.

Plate 31.22   George Cruikshank, The Court at Brighton a la Chinese!, 1816, hand-coloured engraving, British Library, London. Photo: Bridgeman Art Library.

Plate 31.23   *Artist uncertain, possibly W. Heath, New Baubles for the Chinese Temple, 1820, hand-coloured engraving. Photo: courtesy of the Royal Pavilion, Libraries and Museums, Brighton and Hove.*

Plate 32.1   Eugène Delacroix, The Death of Sardanapalus, 1827–8, oil on canvas, 395 × 439 cm, Louvre, Paris. Photo: © RMN/Hervé Lewandowski.

Plate 32.2 Charles-Emile Champmartin, Massacre of the Janissaries, 1828, oil on canvas, 472 × 628 cm, Musée d'art et d'histoire, Rochefort. Photo: reproduced by kind permission of Musée d'art et d'histoire, Rochefort.

Plate 32.3 Jacques-Louis David, *Andromache mourning Hector, 1783, oil on canvas, 275 × 203 cm, Louvre, Paris.*
Photo: © RMN/ R.G. Ojeda.

Plate 32.4 *Jean-Auguste-Dominique Ingres, The Apotheosis of Homer, 1827, 152 × 203 cm, oil on canvas, Louvre, Paris. Photo: © RMN/R.G. Ojeda.*

Plate 32.5 Jacques-Louis David, The Lictors returning to Brutus the Bodies of his Sons, 1789, oil on canvas, 323 × 422 cm, Louvre, Paris.
Photo: © RMN/G. Blot/C. Jean.

Plate 32.7   *Peter Paul Rubens, The Rape of the Daughters of Leucippus, c.1619, oil on canvas,*
222 x 210 cm, Alte Pinakothek, Munich. Photo: Bridgeman Art Library.

Plate 32.6   *Peter Paul Rubens, The Landing of Marie de' Medici at Marseilles,*
3 November 1600, 1622–3, oil on canvas, 394 x 295 cm, Louvre, Paris.
Photo: © RMN/Jean/Lewandowski.

Plate 32.8   Jean–Auguste–Dominique Ingres, La Grande Odalisque, 1814, oil on canvas, 91 × 162 cm, Louvre, Paris. Photo: © RMN/Hervé Lewandowski.

209

Plate 32.9   Eugène Delacroix, sketch for The Death of Sardanapalus, 1826–7, oil on canvas, 81 × 100 cm, Louvre, Paris. Photo: © RMN/J.G. Berizzi.

Plate 32.10 Eugène Delacroix, sketch of a female nude, killed from behind, pastel, red and white chalk on paper, 40 × 27 cm, Louvre, Paris, D.A.G. Photo: © RMN / Arnaudet.

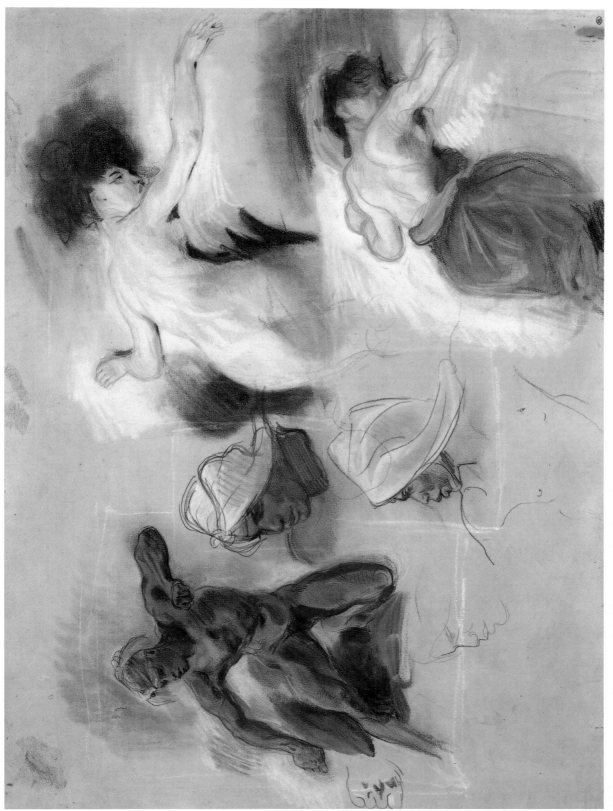

Plate 32.11 Eugène Delacroix, sketch for The Death of Sardanapalus, pastel over graphite, red and white chalk and black crayon on unbleached paper, 44 × 58 cm, Louvre, Paris. Photo: © RMN/Jean Schormans.

212

Plate 32.13   Richard Parkes Bonington, Rouen from the Quays, c.1821, watercolour, British Museum, London. Photo: © British Museum.

Plate 32.12   Eugène Delacroix, Nereid (copy after Peter Paul Rubens), c.1822, oil on canvas, 46.5 × 38 cm, Oeffentliche Kunstsammlung Basel, Kunstmuseum. Photo: Oeffentliche Kunstsammlung Basel/Martin Bühler.

Plate 32.14   Pierre-Narcisse Guérin, The Return of Marcus Sextus, *1799, oil on canvas, 217 x 243 cm, Louvre, Paris. Photo:* © RMN/R.G. Ojeda.

Plate 32.15   Théodore Géricault, The Raft of the Medusa, *1819, oil on canvas, 490 x 716 cm, Louvre, Paris. Photo:* © RMN/Arnaudet.

Plate 32.16 Eugène Delacroix, The Barque of Dante, 1822, oil on canvas, 189 × 246 cm, Louvre, Paris. Photo: © RMN.

Plate 32.17   Nicolas Poussin, A Bacchanalian Revel before a Term, *c.1633, oil on canvas, 99.7 x 142.9 cm, National Gallery, London. Photo: © The National Gallery, London.*

Plate 32.18   Nicolas Poussin, The Rape of the Sabines, *c.1637, 157 x 203 cm, Louvre, Paris. Photo: © RMN/ P. Bernard.*

Plate 32.19   Peter Paul Rubens, The Miracle of St Walburga, c.1610, panel, 75.5 x 98.5 cm, Museum der bildenden Künste, Leipzig.
Photo: © Museum der bildenden Künste, Leipzig/gift of Maximilian Speck von Sternberg.

Plate 32.20   Eugène Delacroix, The Murder of the Bishop of Liège, *1829, oil on canvas 91 x 116 cm, Louvre, Paris. Photo: © RMN/ Hervé Lewandowski.*

Plate 32.21   Eugène Delacroix, sketch for The Murder of the Bishop of Liège, *1827, oil on canvas, 60 x 72.5 cm, Musée des Beaux-Arts de Lyon. Photo: © Studio Basset.*

Plate 32.23   Eugène Delacroix, Portrait of Niccolò Paganini, 1831, oil on cardboard on wood panel, 45 × 30.4 cm, Phillips Collection, Washington, D.C. Photo: courtesy of The Phillips Collection, Washington, D.C.

Plate 32.22   Eugène Delacroix, Michelangelo in his Studio, 1849–50, oil on canvas, 40 × 32 cm, Musée Fabre, Montpellier. Photo: Giraudon/Bridgeman Art Library.

Plate 32.24   Francisco de Goya, They're Hot, *Plate 13 of* Los Caprichos *print series, 1799, etching with aquatint, 21.9 × 15.3 cm, private collection. Photo: Index/Bridgeman Art Library.*

Plate 32.25   Eugène Delacroix, Priests and Monks, *wash, 10.2 x 12.6 cm, Louvre, Paris.*
Photo: © RMN/Michèle Bellot.

Plate 32.26   Eugène Delacroix, sketch after
Goya's Caprichos, c.1824, pen and brown ink
on paper, 22.1 x 18cm, Fogg Art Museum,
Cambridge, MA. Courtesy of Harvard
University Art Museums, bequest of Francis
L. Hofer. Photo: Photographic Services ©
President and Fellows of Harvard College.

Plate 32.27 Eugène Delacroix, Greece on the Ruins of Missolonghi, *1826, oil on canvas, 209 x 147 cm, Musée des Beaux-Arts, Bordeaux. Photo: © M.B.A. de Bordeaux/Lysiane Gauthier.*

Plate 32.28   Eugène Delacroix, Liberty Leading the People, 1830, oil on canvas, 260 x 325 cm, Louvre, Paris. Photo: © RMN/Hervé Lewandowski.

Plate 32.29 *Eugène Delacroix,*
Mephistopheles appears before Faust, *1828,*
lithograph, third of six states, second edition,
© PMVP/Briant.

Plate 32.30 *Eugène Delacroix,* Duel with Valentine, *1828, lithograph, fourth of six states, second edition,*
Bibliothèque nationale de France.

Plate 32.31 *Eugène Delacroix*, Faust and Mephistopheles, *1828, lithograph, fourth of five states, second edition, Bibliothèque nationale de France.*

Plate 32.32 *Eugène Delacroix*, Mephistopheles in the Air, *1828, lithograph, second edition, 27 x 23 cm, Bibliothèque nationale de France.*

Plate 32.33 Eugène Delacroix, Faust attempts to seduce Marguerite, *1828, lithograph, third of six states, second edition, 26.2 x 20.8 cm, Bibliothèque nationale de France.*

Plate 32.34 Eugène Delacroix, Marguerite's Ghost appears to Faust, *1828, lithograph, fifth of six states, second edition, Bibliothèque nationale de France.*

Plate 32.35 Eugène Delacroix, Mephistopheles appears before Faust, *1826–7, exhibited at the Salon of 1827–8, oil on canvas, 46 × 38 cm, Wallace Collection, London. Photo: reproduced by kind permission of the Trustees of the Wallace Collection, London.*

Plate 32.36   Eugène Delacroix, Acrobats' Riding Class, 1822, lithograph, Bibliothèque nationale de France.

Plate 32.37 François Boucher, Leopard Hunt, *1736, oil on canvas, 174 × 129 cm, Musée de Picardie, Amiens.*
Photo: Jean-Marc Manaï.

Plate 32.38   Gold box with painted enamel decoration, Paris: F.-N. Génard, 1761–2, 3.6 × 6.8 × 5.4 cm, Wallace Collection, London.
Photo: reproduced by kind permission of the Trustees of the Wallace Collection, London.

Plate 32.39   Gold box with engraved and enamelled decoration, Paris: Cheval, 1749–50, 3.1 × 7.1 × 5.1 cm, Wallace Collection, London.
Photo: reproduced by kind permission of the Trustees of the Wallace Collection, London.

Plate 32.40 Eugène Delacroix, The Combat of the Giaour and Hassan, 1826, oil on canvas, 59.6 x 73.4 cm, Art Institute of Chicago. Gift of Mrs Bertha Palmer Thorne, Mrs Rose Movius Palmer, Mr and Mrs Arthur M. Wood, Mr and Mrs Gordon Palmer. 1962.966.

Photo: © Art Institute of Chicago.

Plate 32.41   Eugène Delacroix, A Young Tiger playing with its Mother, *1830, oil on canvas, 131 x 194.5 cm, Louvre, Paris. Photo:* © RMN/H. Lewandowski.

Plate 32.42   Eugène Delacroix, Tiger attacking a Wild Horse, *1826–9, watercolour, 17.9 x 24.9 cm, Louvre, Paris. Photo:* © RMN/Michèle Bellot.

Plate 32.43   George Stubbs, Horse attacked by a Lion, *c.1768–9, oil on canvas, 243.8 x 333 cm, Yale Center for British Art, Paul Mellon Collection, New Haven. Photo: Bridgeman Art Library.*

Plate 32.44   Eugène Delacroix, Lion Hunt, *1855, oil on canvas, 56.5 x 73.5 cm, National Museum of Fine Arts, Stockholm. Photo: Hans Thorwid, 1994.*

Plate A3.1   James Gillray, The Zenith of French Glory, *12 February 1793, cartoon, British Museum, London. Photo: by courtesy of the Trustees of the British Museum.*

Plate A3.2   James Gillray, Smelling out a Rat, 3 December 1790, cartoon, 24.8 x 35.1 cm, Smith Collection, British Museum, London. Photo: by courtesy of the Trustees of the British Museum.

Plate A3.3   James Gillray, Substitutes for Bread, 24 December 1795, cartoon, British Museum, London. Photo: by courtesy of the Trustees of the British Museum.

T.French.

A FREEBORN ENGLISHMAN,

the Admiration of the World; the Envy of Surrounding Nations;
&c &c.

Plate A3.4   Thomas Spence, A Freeborn Englishman, *coloured etching, 15.9 x 11.1 cm, British Museum, London. Photo: by courtesy of the Trustees of the British Museum.*

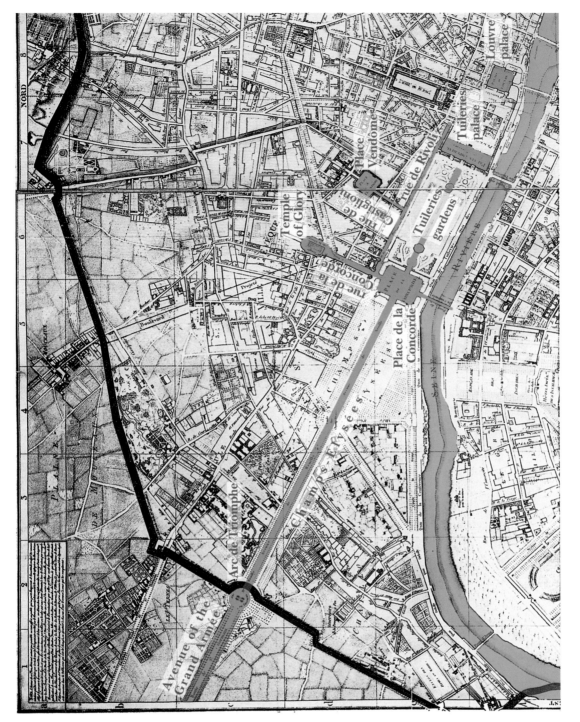

Plate A3.5   Charles Picquet, Plan de la Ville de Paris, 1809, Bibliothèque Nationale de France, Paris.

Plate A3.6 J.F.T. Chalgrin (circle of), design for the Arc de Triomphe, pen and ink on paper, Centre Historique des Archives Nationales, Paris.

Plate A3.7   James Gillray, The King of Brobdingnag and Gulliver, *26 June 1803, cartoon, British Museum, London. Photo: by courtesy of the Trustees of the British Museum.*

Plate V2.1 Francisco de Goya, The Sleep of Reason Produces Monsters, c.1798, *etching with aquatint,*
21.6 x 15.2 cm, Musée des Beaux-Arts, Lille. Photo: © RMN/Quecq d'Henripret.

Plate V2.2   *Francisco de Goya,* Family of Carlos IV, *1800–1, oil on canvas, 280 × 336 cm, Museo del Prado, Madrid. Photo: rights reserved* © *Museo Nacional del Prado, Madrid.*

Plate V2.3   *Francisco de Goya,* Godoy as Commander in the War of the Oranges, *c.1801, 180 × 267 cm, Museo de la Real Academia de Bellas Artes de San Fernando, Madrid. Photo: reproduced by courtesy of Museo de la Real Academia de Bellas Artes de San Fernando.*

Plate V2.4   *Vicente López, Ferdinand VII, 1808–11, 240 × 116 cm, Museo de l'Almodí, Xàtiva.*
Photo: reproduced by courtesy of Museo de l'Almodí, Xàtiva.

Plate V2.5   Francisco de Goya, Second of May 1808, 1814, oil on canvas, 266 x 345 cm, Museo del Prado, Madrid. Photo: rights reserved © Museo Nacional del Prado, Madrid.

244

Plate V2.6 Francisco de Goya, Third of May 1808, 1814, oil on canvas, 266 x 345 cm, Museo del Prado, Madrid. Photo: rights reserved © Museo Nacional del Prado, Madrid.

Plate V2.7 Francisco de Goya, Ferdinand VII in a Royal Mantle, *1814?, oil on canvas, 212 × 146 cm, Museo del Prado, Madrid.* Photo: *rights reserved © Museo Nacional del Prado, Madrid.*

Plate V2.8   Francisco de Goya, Madhouse, c.1816, oil on panel, 45 x 72 cm, Museo de la Real Academia de Bellas Arts de San Fernando, Madrid. Photo: Bridgeman Art Library.

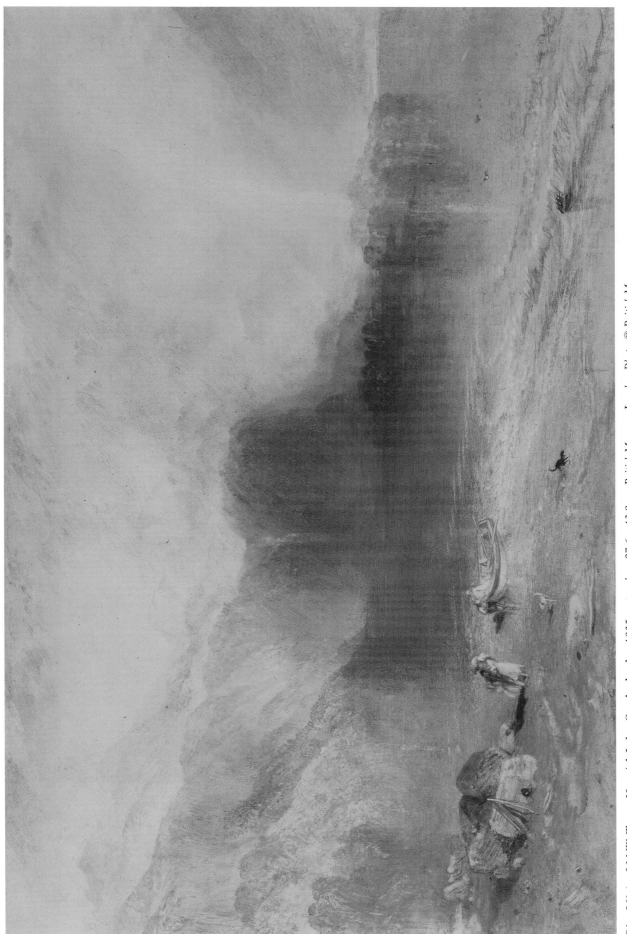

Plate V3.1 J.M.W. Turner, Keswick Lake, Cumberland, c.1835, watercolour, 27.6 x 43.8 cm, British Museum, London. Photo: © British Museum.

Plate V.4.1   Eugène Delacroix, Jewish Wedding in Morocco, 1841, oil on canvas, 105 × 140.5 cm, Louvre, Paris. Photo: Bridgeman Art Library.

Plate V4.2 Eugène Delacroix, *Women of Algiers in their Apartment*, 1834, oil on canvas, 180 x 229 cm, Louvre, Paris. Photo: © RMN/Le Mage.

250

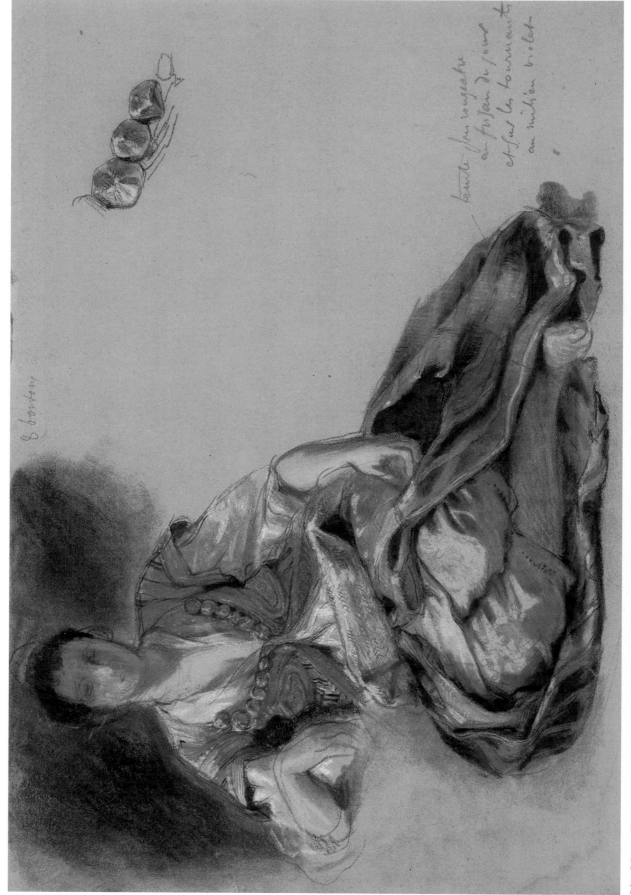

Plate V4.3   Eugène Delacroix, Study for the Women of Algiers, 1834, pastel, 27.5 x 42.4 cm, Louvre, Paris. Photo: © RMN/Michèle Bellot.

Plate V4.4   Eugène Delacroix, Arabs of Oran, *1833, etching, first of six states, 17.3 x 21.4 cm, Bibliothèque nationale de France.*

Plate V4.5   Eugène Delacroix, Clash of Moorish Horsemen, *1834, etching, single state, 18.4 x 25.1 cm, Bibliothèque nationale de France.*

Plate V4.6 Eugène Delacroix, Arab sitting, *drawing in black crayon, 310 × 274 cm, British Museum, London. Photo: © British Museum.*